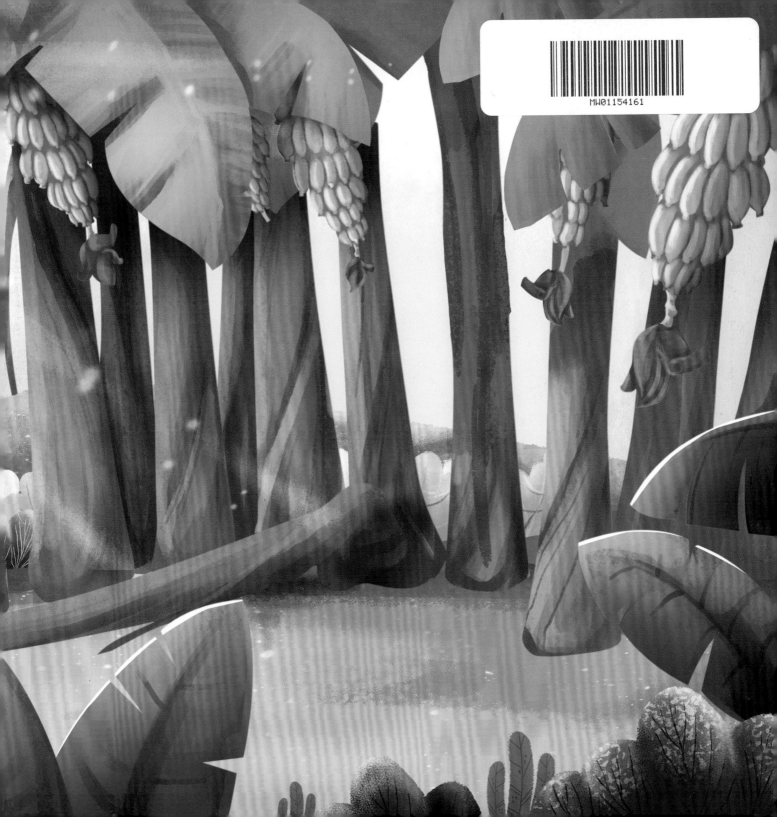

Visit

WWW.YOUNGERMEACADEMY.COM

to request an author visit for your organization, download free
coloring pages, watch free video e-books, and more.

If you enjoy this book, please

LEAVE A REVIEW →

to support our independent family project.

Created by Ben Okon

Illustrated by Khaidir Syafei and CreativeNext

For Matt, a little monkey with a bright future

Special thanks to my dad, my first personal finance coach

Published by Younger Media, LLC
www.youngermeacademy.com
ISBN: 978-1-961428-05-8 (hardcover)
Library of Congress Control Number: 2023910810

On a very fine morning, a monkey named Matt
sat up high in his fort in the trees.
As he chomped on his seventh banana that day,
an unusual sight made him freeze!

A giant blue portal appeared in the trees,
and an old, feeble monkey came out.
"Young Matt, oh hello! I'm you—Future Matt,"
the old monkey announced with a shout.

"Young Matt, I'm in need of your help right away,
'cause your future is looking quite bleak.
I'm old and I'm thin and I can't climb a tree.
I'm so terribly hungry and weak."

The younger Matt said, "Oh how awful, my friend,"
as he tossed back another used peel.
"Don't you worry, old pal, I have plenty of chow!
You can eat here with me for a meal."

"That's not what I need," Old Matt said with a sigh as he drooled at the food in the tree.
"**You** need to help solve this problem for good, for the sake of your future . . . for ME!"

"Young Matt, I was you, so I already know
that you find ten bananas per day.
I know that it's tempting to gobble them all,
but I've learned of a much better way.

My friends in the future who eat really well
didn't eat each banana they found.
They saved one or two that they didn't then eat
and they planted their seeds in the ground."

Young Matt said, "That's silly. I've tried it before!
Some simply would not become trees.
I don't want to risk my bananas at all.
I'll eat every one if I please!"

"That isn't the point!" the old monkey replied.
"You don't need all the fruit seeds to grow!
Even if only a few become trees,
your pantry will still overflow!"

Tree Graveyard
for Compost

"You see, one banana grows into a tree that will give you bananas galore!
So even if some of them don't become trees, those that do will keep giving you more!

You'll soon have much more than your ten fruits a day.
Eleven or twelve might then grow!
You can then eat your ten and still plant some again,
you really will reap what you sow!"

"That's great!" Young Matt said. "But we missed something big. There are monkeys all over the land!

With the giant new stash of bananas I make,
I can give them a big helping hand!"

"When I find my ten fruits in the trees every day,
I will promptly go plant the first two.
Then I'll give out a few to some monkeys in need,
and I'll still have a bunch left to chew!"

"That's spot on!" Old Matt said, "You won't notice they're gone. It'll pretty much feel like right now . . .

. . . but in a few years, you will cry happy tears with your freshly picked mountain of chow!"

"I love this new plan!" Young Matt said as he dreamed.
"I'll get started on this by next year!"

"Free to all who need"

Banana bread - FREE
Banana pudding - FREE
Banana shakes - FREE
Banana pizza - FREE
Banana splits - FREE

Matt followed the plan and he planted his trees.
Pretty soon, he was swimming in fruit!
Then he started to feed all the monkeys in need
from cabanas stuffed full of his loot.

Several years later, the portal reopened,
and Future Matt came once again.
He said to Young Matt, "Thanks for helping me out
by planting bananas back then!"

Future Matt looked so great! He was happy and strong!
Said Young Matt, "I'm so glad you're not blue!

Of course I helped out, for without any doubt,
what's important to me . . . is YOU!"

"OLDER ME" ACADEMY

(More about Personal Finance for adults and advanced readers)

Managing money is for adults . . . or is it? By age 7, many children begin to solidify basic habits, like conservation and delayed gratification, that can impact their long term financial behaviors. When nurtured into adulthood, these habits can translate into financial stability even without advantages like high income or inherited wealth.

So, how can you start on your path to financial security? Well, as billionaire Warren Buffett said, "Someone's sitting in the shade today because someone planted a tree a long time ago." Most advisors recommend that you plant your trees for the future by following four principles:

- **Don't borrow too many bananas.** Pay credit card bills on time and avoid debt with high interest rates. Instead, set up an emergency bank account that you can use to "borrow" money from yourself for urgent needs.

- **Save bananas.** When you get money, send as much as you can afford to save into a separate account before you have a chance to use it. Many banks or employers can do this for you automatically. You can start small if needed, then aim for more as time goes on!

- **Plant your trees.** Instead of keeping your savings in a regular bank account, grow them by moving your money to a diversified investment account. You can learn about investments yourself, or start by finding a robo-advisor that can do it for you at almost no cost.

- **Start planting early.** When invested responsibly, money grows a lot over time. For example, putting money in an investment account that grows at the average rate of the market (~8% growth per year) would grow by 10 times after 30 years. This sounds fantastic (and it is!), but it would have grown by 20 times if you had invested it just 10 years earlier!

Financial security and discipline are so much easier to achieve when you start young, so why not build good habits together as a family? For example, a $6 allowance could be split into $3 for spending, $1 for charity, and $2 for investing.

Future Matt would be proud,
and Future You will thank you!

Fun fact: Most grocery store bananas won't grow when planted—but wild ones will!

THE STORY BEHIND YOUNGER ME ACADEMY

Great children's books create special moments that can be shared across generations.

I realized this when my grandmother Gigi, a retired writing teacher, became isolated during COVID-19 with no way to meet my new baby Judah. Instead, we connected over video, where we enjoyed reading Judah's books together.

These moments we shared—the three of us, across nearly 100 years of age—were special, but usually not because of the books. Most books were written for *Judah* without reaching out to pull *me* into his moment as well. They taught him the ABC's, showed him pictures of new things, and told him stories about sharing and friendship.

But I wanted a book that I could learn from, too. In particular, I wanted to learn things that I wished I had learned when I was younger, so that Judah and I could grow together. I began writing my own books, and the *Younger Me Academy* was born. Each book is designed to:

- **Help anybody of any age learn and grow** with simplified life-long lessons from science, psychology, business, and beyond.

- **Pull everyone in** (including older readers and younger listeners) through vividly illustrated, character-driven stories written with rhythm and rhyme.

- **Create a deep, special moment** between easily-distracted kids and parents with stories that are long enough to savor but short enough to finish in one fun read.

Younger Me Academy is dedicated to Gigi. Through her writing, teaching, and stories, she inspired me to be a better father, husband, friend, professional, and human. My dream is that this series can continue her legacy by helping other growth-oriented families and their "Younger Me's" to do the same.

Thanks for reading. Please support this independent family project by leaving a book review wherever you found *Younger Me Academy*. I love to learn from you too, so I read every single one.

Ben

Ben Okon is a father who never outgrew his childhood habit of asking "why?" and "how?" Now that he has to be the one giving the answers, he loves challenging himself to think through the things he wishes he had known earlier in life from the perspective of a child.

In his spare time, Ben is a business leader who has developed people, product, and corporate strategies with companies like Google, Bain & Co., and Starwood Hotels. He holds an MBA from the Wharton School of Business at the University of Pennsylvania and a BS from the School of Hotel Administration at Cornell University.